Design Your Dream
Wedding Rings

From Engagement to Eternity

Calla Gold

CGJ Media

Santa Barbara, California

Design Your Dream Wedding Rings: From Engagement to Eternity

Published by CGJ Media an imprint of Carp House Press

CGJ Media
P.O. Box 40102
Santa Barbara, CA 93140
805.963.4157

www.callagold.com

Copyright © 2019 Calla Gold

All designs are the intellectual property of designer/author Calla Gold and Calla Gold Jewelry.

Photography provided by Calla Gold.

ISBN 978-0-9860663-1-3 print
ISBN 978-0-9860663-2-0 ebook

LCCN Library of Congress Control Number: 2018905097

All rights reserved under International and Pan-American Copyright Conventions. No portion of this book may be reproduced in any form without permission in writing from CGJ Media, except by a newspaper or magazine reviewer who wishes to quote brief passages in a review.

Publisher's Cataloging-In-Publication Data
(Prepared by The Donohue Group, Inc.)

Names: Gold, Calla.
Title: Design your dream wedding rings : from engagement to eternity / Calla Gold.
Description: Santa Barbara, California : CGJ Media, [2019] | Includes index.
Identifiers: ISBN 9780986066313 (print) | ISBN 9780986066320 (ebook)
Subjects: LCSH: Wedding rings—Design. | Engagement rings—Design. | Diamond jewelry—Design. | Jewelry settings.
Classification: LCC NK7445 .G65 2019 (print) | LCC NK7445 (ebook) | DDC 739.27/82—dc23

Content Editor: Christine Casey Logsdon, RCGC, Inc.
Art Director: Penelope C. Paine, To Press and Beyond
Copy Editor: Gail Kearns, To Press and Beyond
Typography and Layout: Christine Nolt, Cirrus Book Design

10 9 8 7 6 5 4 3 2 1

Printed in United States of America

*To my husband, Jeremy Gold,
my son Dan and nephews Alex and Brennan,
who helped me with my first book. And to my clients whose
dream rings I share to inspire the next dreamers.*

Contents

Preface xi

SECTION ONE: Learning the Language of Rings 1

What Jewelers Say 2
Why I Wrote This Book, Felicia's Story 3
The Sixteen Steps to the Perfect Ring 4
Sixteen Steps to Custom Jewelry Design 4
A Splash of Color in a Diamond Field 7
Ring Basics 9
Gemstone Basics 10
Diamond Shapes to Consider 11
   Fancy or Non-Round Cut Diamonds 11
   More Square Shapes 12
Diamond Shapes and Your Hand—
   Three Stories, Kaitlyn, Romana, and Silvana 12
Engagement Rings, Wedding Rings, and Wedding Bands 14
The Engagement and Wedding Ring Set 14
   The Engagement Ring 15
   The Wedding Band 17
Diamond and Gem Wedding Band Styles 18
Contoured Wedding Rings/Bands 19
The Eternity Band 20
Stacking Bands 21
The Anniversary Band 23
Wedding Jewelry for the LGBTQ Community 24

Section Two: Ring Settings — 27
    What Works for You? — 28
    Prong Setting — 29
    Head Setting — 29
    Bezel Setting — 30
    Channel Setting — 31
    Inlay Setting — 32
    Flush Setting — 33
    Pavé Setting — 34
    Randi's Collection of Auntie's Sapphires — 35

Section Three: Choosing the Right Ring — 37
    The First Priority for Your Ring: Make Your Hand Look Good — 38
    Ideal Shapes and Details: Discover Your Best Ring Look — 39
    The Second Priority for Your Ring: Hold Up to Your Lifestyle and Roll with the Punches — 40
    Tina's Choice, and Second Thoughts — 41
    Elements to Consider When Choosing a Ring Design for Your Best Look — 42
    Choosing Your Best Metal — 45
    White Gold vs. Platinum — 45
    Should You Choose Rose Gold for Your Wedding Ring? — 47
    Titanium, Tungsten, and Alternate Metal Wedding Bands — 49
        Your Magic Ring! — 49
    Gold and Platinum Rings Can Be Sized and Soldered — 51

Section Four: Decorative Extras — 53
    Inscription vs. Decorative Engraving — 54

Three Types of Engraving: Hand, Machine, and Laser	55
Hand Engraving	55
Machine Engraving	56
Laser Engraving	57
Design Choices and Metal Engraving Techniques	58
Milgrain Edging	58
Cast-In Engraving	59
For a Deeper and Bolder Engraved Look	59
Finishing Techniques That Can Make Your Ring Look Stellar	60
Choosing Textures and Finishes to Add Personality to Your Design	60
Hammer Finish	60
Matte Finish	61
Satin Finish	62
Stipple Finish	62
High Polish	62
Oxidation	62
Enamel	63
Twig Finish	63
Plating, the Secret Technique That Can Elevate Your Ring	64
Rhodium	64
Black Rhodium Plating	65
Can You Black Up Your Wedding Ring?	66
Alternatives When You Want Dark Gray or Black Details	66
Yellow Gold Plating	67
Rose Gold Plating	67
Two-Tone Rings and Plating	68
Plating and Your Ring's Maintenance	69

SECTION FIVE: Redesigning from an Existing Ring — 71
   Why Redesign? — 72
   Carol's Redesign — 72
   Julie's Wedding Ring from Grandma's Diamonds — 74
   Christine and Sam's 25th Wedding Anniversary Redesign — 75
   Marlo and Ben and the Family Diamonds — 76

SECTION SIX: CADs and Waxes, What You Need to Know — 79
   Creating Your Design Concept, Making Your Dream Ring Reality — 80
   The Drawings… — 80
   The CAD… Computer-Aided Design — 81
      Hand Wax Models — 82
   Six Features to Look for in a Wax or CAD Model — 83
   Final Words on What You Are Looking For — 85

SECTION SEVEN: All about Your Hands — 87
   Getting Your Finger Sized, the Right Way — 88
   Wide Band Ring Sizers vs. Narrow Band Ring Sizers—
      They Make the Difference — 89
   Four Things Not to Do before You Get Your Finger
      Measured for Size — 90
   Five Reasons Why You Still Might Get a Wrong Size — 90
   Fit Feel, What's Too Tight and What's Too Loose? — 91
      Guys, Resist the Urge to Go Loose in Your Ring Size — 91
      Figuring Out Your Girlfriend's Finger Size — 92
   Don't Despair, Solutions for Rings That Spin and Big Knuckles — 94
      Lori's Wedding Ring Dilemma — 95
      Is This You? — 95

Three Solutions	96
Other Options: Horseshoes and Squares	97
Which Solution Is Right for You?	98
It's Your Dream, You Deserve to Wear It	98
Epilogue	99
Your Dream Made Real	100
Appendix	101
Quiz about Your Wedding Band for the Guys	103
Quiz about Your Engagement Ring Design for the Women	105
About the Author	109
Acknowledgments	111
Photo Credits	111
Index	113

Extra Information

You'll notice purple boxes throughout the book offering additional information. These refer to blog posts on my website. These blog posts offer additional pictures or otherwise expand on what's being discussed in the book. I created a page at callagold.com/book-info with a list of live links corresponding to each page in the book.

Calla's Blog
How to Choose a Jeweler—16 Questions to Ask Yourself

"A jeweler's job is to balance your visions with what works with your lifestyle."

Preface

This book was written to help you clearly communicate your jewelry design dream to your jewelry maker.

I've been a jeweler in Santa Barbara, California since 1983. I've been speaking and educating about jewelry and design since the 1990s and blogging jewelry design since 2008. When I first started designing jewelry, my favorite part was creating the special details my clients dreamed up to symbolize the quirky, romantic, and historic aspects of their relationships.

I want you to love your jewelry and I want you to love the part you had in its creation. I want you to be proud of your ring because it's unique.

With just a little language of jewelry, you'll have the information you need to talk to your jeweler, and make sure she or he understands your vision. And creates that vision for you.

May your jewelry be as individual as you are.

Calla Gold

Section One

Learning the Language of Rings

What Jewelers Say

The way we jewelers talk about jewelry design is similar whether it's a ring, a pendant, a necklace, a bracelet, or earrings. Because of that, in this book I chose to focus on your "dream rings" with special emphasis on wedding rings. But everything you learn here will help you design any piece of jewelry. As you'll see later, "a prong is a prong is a prong."

Most well-prepared brides know what they want in a ring, but they don't always know how to articulate it. They often bring a file of details to show me, either on their computer or in a scrapbook of pictures torn from brides' magazines, or pictures on their iPad or cell phone.

Why I Wrote This Book, Felicia's Story

Felicia arrived at our first meeting, sat down on the chair next to me, and opened up her laptop.

"These engraving styles are exactly what I want," she said, pointing to two rings I had designed. A couple of minutes later, she told me she "for sure wanted a 'roundy square' diamond."

"Cushion cut?" I asked, showing her a picture.

"That's it!"

Then she said, "I want my diamond set in those "sticky-uppy things."

"You mean prongs?" I asked.

"Yes, prongs," she replied with a smile.

Felicia's reply wasn't unique, but she did give me a gift. In my mind I saw a book, *Design Your Dream Wedding Rings*. It would have photos explaining, naming, and showing different setting styles and options. I wanted to dedicate this book it to her and every woman or man eager to create their perfect piece of jewelry.

When you're explaining what you want in a ring to a jeweler, it's easy for details to get missed. Unless we're speaking the same language, you might end up with a beautiful, but altered version of your idea. This can lead to a sense of loss, because the finer details aren't quite what you wanted.

I don't want that to happen to you.

The Sixteen Steps to the Perfect Ring

It can be helpful to know the steps you'll be embarking on when journeying toward that special ring. Knowing the steps allows you to choose how prepared you want to be, knowing that your jeweler will help fill in a lot of the blanks.

Find a jeweler you feel comfortable with before you start your journey. If you aren't sure how to go about finding the right jeweler for you, you can read my blog post, "How to Choose a Jeweler."

Sixteen Steps to Custom Jewelry Design

The following steps will help you to collaborate with your jeweler.

1. Look at pictures of jewelry you like in magazines and online. Keep notes in a folder of features that appeal to you. When possible, take pictures of details you admire. Think about what kinds of gemstones you like.

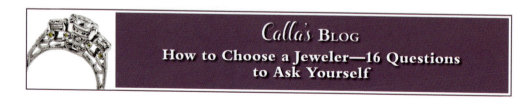

Calla's BLOG
How to Choose a Jeweler—16 Questions to Ask Yourself

2. Discuss the project with your jeweler. Share your folder of notes. Point out things you like, details that appeal to you, and gemstones that pique your interest. Knowing *exactly* what you want is not important at this point. Pay attention to themes: vintage versus modern; detailed versus simple; rustic and hand-hewn, or sleek and spare; diamonds versus colored gemstones; gold or platinum. Add to your folder of pictures as you go along. Discuss your budget with your jeweler.

3. Try on different styles of rings. See what widths and heights are most flattering to your fingers and hand. Get a feel for what's comfortable. Consider wear and maintenance issues too. Some metals and gemstones withstand more rigorous lifestyles than others.

4. Have your jeweler sketch out a preliminary drawing once you've decided on a design.

5. Discuss the drawing and make modifications as needed. Include exact measurements (and your finger size!).

6. Approve the drawing.

7. Get a bid from your jeweler for the entire project. This should include a written description of the work to be done, the drawing, and the cost of materials, CAD (computer-aided design), wax model creation, and labor.

8. Approve the project. Normally, a down payment is requested by the jeweler.

9. Have your jeweler create a CAD or wax model of the ring. Review pictures of the CAD or finished wax model and request any refinements or modifications. Approve the CAD or wax model.

10. Choose your gemstones with your jeweler.

11. Your ring is cast in your chosen metal.

12. All gemstones are set.

13. Textures, special features, and engraving are applied.

14. Your ring is polished and given its final touches.

15. Make sure you like your ring. Pay attention to size, finish, edges, settings, gemstones, etc. Have your jeweler make any needed adjustments.

16. Approve your custom new ring! Put it on. Smile.

The steps aren't carved in stone. Sometimes they get reversed. Occasionally, substeps will be added, or a step isn't needed, but you get the idea. Right?

For more detailed dives into different steps, check out my gigantic blog post, "Breaking Down Homework for Your Design Idea." This post will show you how to focus on the actions you care about most.

A Splash of Color in a Diamond Field

Watch a bunch of movies and you'd think that every woman wears a solitaire for her engagement ring and a plain gold band for her wedding ring. But most people, given a little time to imagine, have far more exciting ideas about the ring they want to look down at for the rest of their lives.

Diamonds are the reigning goddesses of gemstones, especially for wedding rings. They're the hardest of the jewelry gemstones, so they'll stand the test of decades of wear. They also stubbornly sparkle even when they collect lotion or hard water deposits. And who doesn't think love should sparkle?

I've written a number of posts about the importance of the four Cs—cut, color, clarity, and carat weight—that you can read for more information. I recommend that you start with "Choosing Diamond Color."

Calla's Blog
Choosing Diamond Color, How to Shop Right for Diamond Color

Some women see color in their wedding set too. If you decide that you don't want a diamond as your center gemstone, choose a strong gemstone.

Tsavorite after four years of daily wear.

Everyday wear can scratch, chip, or break many less resilient gemstones. The sapphire family is the hardest gemstone after the diamond—and diamonds today come in a range of colors.

You may have a favorite gemstone that isn't in the sapphire or diamond family. If you're thinking of softer gemstones, I urge you to read "Diamonds vs. Forbidden Wedding Ring Gemstones."

After re-faceting to remove facet abrasions.

Calla's Blog
Diamonds vs. Forbidden Wedding Ring Gemstones

Ring Basics

If you're already familiar with the basic parts of a ring, skip on ahead. If you aren't, this is a great time to learn the most important words a jeweler will use when discussing the elements of your dream ring.

Prongs are the claw-like arms that hold gems in place. (I'll talk about these and other settings later in the book.)

The *center stone* is the featured gemstone, usually the biggest and most exposed to wear and tear.

Side stones are middle-sized gemstones compared to the center gemstone.

The ring's *crown* is the central, top element of the ring. It is the part that is designed to hold the main gemstones. The easiest way is to think of it as the star of the ring. The crown is generally the top third of the ring with the main design and gemstones.

The *shank* is that part of the ring that surrounds the finger, connected to the crown. It can be the plain shiny part beyond the main gemstones or it can be set with gems. We talk about the shank to figure out how wide we want it, or how thick it should be, or where the engraving should go.

Accent stones are those that are set into the ring's *shank*.

Another important part of the ring is the *gallery,* the side view under the central gems. This area offers an opportunity for beautiful detail, simple or complex.

There are as many details as there are ring ideas, but these are the basics that let you and your jeweler start a conversation that will lead you to the design you want.

Gemstone Basics

I want to give you the same overview for gemstones that I just did for rings. Skip ahead if you're a jewelry pro.

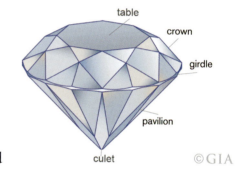

You can see the main parts of a faceted gemstone in this drawing. The table is the biggest facet, the one you'll look down at when the stone is set in your ring. The girdle is the widest part of the gemstone, where prongs or other setting styles hold it in place. The culet is the pointy bottom of the gemstone that is protected within the ring setting.

Now you have the basics of settings and gemstones. Jewelers will use this language to talk about any specific part of the piece of jewelry you want to create. It's most important when talking about wedding and engagement rings, because for many people that is the most precious jewelry purchase they will ever make.

Diamond Shapes to Consider

You may have asked yourself, "What diamond shape should I get?" or "Will a particular diamond shape look better on my hand?" There are a lot of shape choices, but you might be interested to know a big reason for different shaped diamonds.

Round Cut
© GIA

The raw, out-of-the-ground diamonds, lend themselves to a round, brilliant cut because of their shape. Diamond cutters like to use as much of the rough diamond as possible and the round cut achieves this.

Since diamonds are sold by weight, diamond cutters will try to use the maximum amount of the rough in their cutting of a diamond.

Oval Shape
© GIA

Fancy or Non-Round Cut Diamonds

Inclusions that are visible to the eye can occur in a rough diamond that would ruin the beauty of a round, brilliant-cut diamond. If that same piece of rough was cut as a marquis or a pear shape, the diamond cutter could possibly avoid that annoying big black carbon inclusion. In this way, the "fancy" cut diamonds were born.

Pear Shape
© GIA

The symmetry and sparkle in a round, brilliant-cut diamond gives fantastic light return, a measurement used to quantify how sparkly (yeah, that's a technical term) your diamond is.

In comparison, a pear-cut diamond with less symmetry will give a subtler light return.

Heart Cut
© GIA

More Square Shapes

In response to the appeal of the emerald cut, but the poorer light return numbers due to fewer facets, diamond cutters came up with cushion cuts, square modified brilliants and other square and rectangular shaped cuts with more facets that gave better light return.

Emerald Cut

As diamond lovers are given more choices, it's good for them to know that with fancy cuts can come caveats.

For example, some marquis cut diamonds can have what is called a bow-tie effect. A black area not unlike the shape of a bow-tie that does not return light effectively, but like tiny black holes just sucks it up and beams it into another dimension. I learned that on *Star Trek*.

Diamond Shapes and Your Hand— Three Stories, Kaitlyn, Romana, and Silvana

I've noticed that diamond shapes can make a difference on your hand, and with your chosen design style.

Kaitlyn and Short Fingers

One of my clients, Kaitlyn, had fairly short fingers and many rings seemed to overwhelm her hand.

Marquise Cut
© GIA

We finally tried a marquis cut diamond and it made her fingers look longer. We designed a ring around the marquis and it looked markedly better than round brilliant, cushion, or even oval, which was her runner-up shape choice.

Romana and Her Baby Hands

Romana had been teased for having "baby hands". Her ring finger size was 3¾. A lot of the rings she tried on made her feel like she was playing dress-up in her mom's jewelry box.

Cushion Cut
© GIA

Cushion cut was the style for her. Somehow the squarer proportions gave gravitas (seriousness, adult-y-ness) to her hand. We scaled the ring for her tiny hands, used the cushion cut center diamond and all anyone said was not "baby hands" but "beautiful," "congratulations," and "OMG, I love your ring." We were good with that.

Sylvana and Her Generously Full Hands

Sylvana had slightly puffy fingers. We're all different. She'd tried a lot of rings and diamond shapes and it just clicked when she put on an angular ring with a princess cut diamond on it.

The angularity of the diamond nicely opposed the generous curvy vibe of her hand. It was definitely love. We all agreed that princess cut was her perfect diamond shape.

Princess Cut
© GIA

Calla's Comment

I could go on about all the different shapes that have been perfect for different people, but round brilliant reigns supreme for popularity and availability. Round brilliant also seems to sparkle most when challenged by soap, lotion, and life. You'll always have the greatest amount of selection when you choose round brilliant.

Pick the shape that complements your hand and pick the diamond that sparkles and speaks to you.

Engagement Rings, Weddings Rings, and Wedding Bands

Two Ring Wedding Set

Calla's Comment

In the 1400s, Archduke Maximilian of Austria popularized the idea of engagement rings by proposing to Mary of Burgundy, sending a betrothal ring via courier to her residence in France. The ring he chose was set with flat pieces of diamond creating the letter M.

A lot of people, especially men, are confused about the difference between engagement rings, wedding rings, wedding bands, who gives which to whom, and more important, when to give it. It's a mystery I'm here to help you solve right now.

THE ENGAGEMENT AND WEDDING RING SET

When most people think of "the rings," they're thinking of the engagement ring plus the rings the couple exchange on their wedding day. The woman's wedding set shown above is what you might think of when you imagine "her rings."

Wedding-day rings these days can be so much more. Modern materials, gemstones, engraving, and finishing techniques offer couples more choices and greater opportunities to let their rings make a personal statement.

The Engagement Ring

Terrified of buying the ring? I get it. I don't talk much about actual *purchasing* in this book, but with an engagement ring, the surprise of "popping the question" is often a big part of the deal.

The secret too many people don't know? You pick the *diamond*, not the setting, for your potential bride. It's that easy.

A simple diamond solitaire setting to hold the diamond you have chosen makes a nice placeholder for the purpose of your proposal.

After the proposal, tell your fiancée you want her engagement ring to reflect her taste and to be the ring she wears with pride and passion for the rest of her life. Let her be a part of her engagement ring design.

Those of you who know your potential fiancée's tastes and feel brave enough to propose with a ring you designed, go for it! That design will become part of her proposal story and mean so much.

You're allowed to design. But you aren't *required* to design. You can just as easily let her create her dream ring with the diamond you proposed with.

Diamonds Pavé Set

The engagement ring historically has a large central diamond as the focal point and a simple or complex design around it.

Engagement rings are still offered as a "troth," a pledge of loyalty and faithfulness. And we accept them because we're saying *yes;* we're accepting that pledge. No matter how modern the times or how boundless your options with your rings today, that romantic and meaningful promise remains the reason your engagement ring matters.

Calla's Comment

Some women choose to wear just one ring throughout their married life. While they are engaged, that ring is their engagement ring. After they are married, that same ring merely changes in symbolism.

Your ring whether purchased premade or custom designed must be made to last. It needs to follow the "Four Pillars of a Daily Wear Ring."

A soldered together circle of tin will get the job done as an engagement ring, just as long as your fiancée has a great sense of humor and the real ring is in your other pocket.

Calla's Blog
Wedding Jewelry vs. Occasional Jewelry: Four Pillars of a Daily Wear Ring

The Wedding Band

The word "band" means something distinct to a jeweler: It's the same width all the way around. A man's wedding band is usually always the same width all the way around. The groom receives his wedding band when he marries.

Things jewelers say, "Do you want a band style or more of a ring?" Translation, "Do you want it the same width all the way around or something with different width, top, and bottom sections?"

The top wedding set pictured shows a client's halo style rose gold and diamond wedding set, and her husband's rose and white gold wedding band.

The engagement ring is the one with the big diamond.

For daily wear, a ring must be made robustly, with depth and enough gold or platinum to last for years. A man's band should have some heft to it, as the fellas can be pretty hard on them, and too lightweight a band will bend, or crack, and let him down.

Do read my post on comfort fit, Comfort Fit Ring vs. Flat Fit, Wedding Bands for Comfort, as it is an important element in your fella's willingness to wear his wedding band daily.

Calla's BLOG
Comfort Fit Ring vs. Flat Fit, Wedding Bands for Comfort

Diamond and Gem Wedding Band Styles

I'm often asked about wedding band choices. "Should it be plain like my fiancé's wedding band will be?" or "Since a straight band doesn't look good with my engagement ring, what should I do?" or "I have short fingers, can I even carry a wedding band with my engagement ring?" or "Because of my work I'll probably wear the wedding band more than the engagement ring. How can I make sure that it'll look, you know, wedding-y?"

These are great questions a good designing jeweler can help with. I love to see detail in women's wedding bands, like the sparkle of little diamonds, or the flourish of hand engraving.

Two styles of wedding bands represent the majority of straight wedding band choices for women. Eternity bands are more gem-heavy, and can also stand alone well when you aren't wearing your engagement ring. The stackers style is often thinner and has fewer gemstones.

> ### Calla's COMMENT
> When you start wearing your engagement ring, it is fantastic fun. Don't forget to plan and choose or design your wedding bands. Time flies and it's much better if it flies with your wedding jewelry all figured out than stressing you two weeks before the ceremony.

Contoured Wedding Rings/Bands

In answer to the women who have tried on straight wedding bands and seen that they do not work with the design of their engagement ring, I recommend a contoured wedding band. These are custom made to follow the contours of your engagement ring.

Another option is to choose a wedding ring with an interesting design that though it doesn't lay perfectly with the engagement ring, looks good when worn together. There may be a gap, but it looks fine. Having a gap or two between your engagement and wedding band may just give you the eclectic look you connect with.

Katryn's Contoured Wedding Band

Katryn loved her sapphire and diamond engagement ring. It shouted, I am cherished. However, after she got married, her career in social work started to include home visits. Wearing her engagement ring was not an option. She chose to wear her curved wedding band alone instead.

Katryn knew her job would at some point go in this direction and she'd planned her curved wedding band ahead of time so it could be worn alone.

As beautiful as it is to wear your wedding set together, it is extra special when either of your wedding rings can stand alone.

Make sure your fingers are comfortable with the height and setting style when you choose an eternity-style wedding band.

The Eternity Band

This band style has gemstones, usually diamonds, going all the way around the ring. "I love you for eternity" is the meaning behind the eternity band.

Rings love to orbit your finger. The more gemstones you have set on the band, the less you'll fuss with the ring, trying to keep the gems on top. Eternity bands are wonderful because even as your ring turns around on your finger, the beautiful gems always face up.

Before you commit yourself to this design style, though, be aware that the side-feel (how the ring feels against the surrounding fingers) is often rougher and thicker.

Channel set style is smooth to your fingers on this three-fourths eternity band.

Many of my clients choose a three-fourths eternity band simply to avoid certain maintenance issues that come with a full eternity band.

If you plan to wear this style on a daily basis, make sure that the ring is sturdy, with plenty of metal and not too delicate. These are beautiful and tempting styles, but some of them are designed only for occasional wear.

It will break your heart having to spend more time getting your ring fixed than being able to wear it. Have your eternity band custom-made just for you, taking into account your lifestyle, how often you're going to wear it, and how comfortable you need it to be. You want to figure out how you get the look you want with the function and comfort you need.

STACKING BANDS

Stacking bands, or stackers, are worn in multiples, stacked next to each other. Stackers come in many different types. They can be eternity, with gems all around or more commonly one third to a half way around with gemstones. What makes stacking "stacking" is that you wear similar rings stacked together.

A comfortable ring can be created using very small gemstones, and you won't even feel the gemstones because the ring is so low to the finger.

Three Eternity Bands

You can stack more rings because they are so thin. Many of my clients regularly wear five stacked rings together and they look fantastic.

When planning wedding stackers, I recommend starting with a pair of matching diamond stacking rings. That way two of the same color and style can flank a central engagement ring. Then, when they want a more low-key look to their wedding set—say for traveling—they wear the stackers around a smaller, low-set ring, leaving their engagement ring safely at home.

Hattie's Bonus Ring

I'd taken apart Hattie's impractical and dated ring, made a ring for her daughter-in-law that she loved and we had a few sapphires and diamonds left over. We created this airy wider stacking band, which looks amazing with flanking stackers to set it off.

The Anniversary Band

An anniversary band is traditionally given as an anniversary gift. Its meaning is clear: "I'd marry you all over again."

While this band isn't really a "wedding style" ring, you'll often design this ring to complement your wedding set. The thing that makes it an anniversary band to a jeweler is that the gemstones go only one third to half way down the ring.

Historically, men gave anniversary bands to their wives. But it's a new, more equal world. Husbands' hands look beautiful in anniversary bands too.

Calla's Comment

Joe had designed an engagement ring for his wife that they both loved. Mostly for financial reasons they decided to use his grandmother's wedding band for Ronit's wedding band. The two rings really didn't go together. We designed a ring to pair beautifully with Ronit's engagement ring for their second anniversary. It was an anniversary band that became her wedding band. His gift was a huge improvement on the mismatched heirloom ring.

I just wanted you to know that the anniversary band can be made to be part of a wedding set after the fact or worn on the right hand.

Wedding Jewelry for the LGBTQ Community

Wearing wedding rings is a celebration. In the LGBTQ community, I believe this has never been truer. In my blog post, "LGBTQ Wedding Bands: What About the Guys?" I share a story about Hal and Rick.

A rebel and a gardener, prepping to adopt and making their new home handicapped friendly, they were rushing their wedding ring choices and planning to just do two plain matching bands. That wasn't who they were and happily we talked and they came up with wonderful and individual band designs.

While many gay couples choose traditional wedding band sets, I'm a fan of not being matchy. If you want rings that are unique to each individual in the marriage, there's plenty of room to find a unifying theme to tie your unique rings together.

Hal and Rick's wedding bands share a design element that unifies their symbol of marriage while complementing their individual personalities and hands.

Diane and Laura each had a vision of a perfect wedding ring, but wanted to be sure their rings symbolized their togetherness. Princess (square-cut) diamond gemstones unify their wedding set while the design of the rings expresses their individuality.

Willa Kveta Photography

Calla's Blog
LGBT Wedding Bands — What about the Guys?

Section Two

Ring Settings

What Works for You?

The challenge of the century for me was Dorinne's wedding ring. Her fiancé had designed a ring that turned out to be like a battleship. It had a lot of angles, stood up high and flopped around, and was a bit unfortunate looking.

She wore it for a while and finally said, "Honey, it's hurting me and I really wanted something more feminine and girly."

He said, "Pick out something you love baby-cakes." Fleeing from angles, she picked an airy confection with delicate wires and tiny prong-set diamonds, sprinkled, "like stars in heaven." Unfortunately, it dropped diamonds like a rain cloud.

Dorinne was referred to me three weeks before the ceremony. She needed a ring and fast. It turned out that her taste and her lifestyle were black and white. She loves her ring that we made, even though it isn't frilly and girly. It is feminine and strong and has smartly set little diamonds.

I'm sharing Dorinne's story so you'll think about how your lifestyle will impact the design choices you make. This next section will show with pictures all the different types of setting styles you have to choose from for your dream ring.

Prong Setting

A prong setting, sometimes called a claw setting, uses three or more small, finger-like extensions that securely hold the gemstone in place. The prong setting is the most commonly used gemstone setting style, particularly for the solitaire design (only one gemstone on a plain thin band).

Whether they rise from a simple band or come up from a complex design involving other gemstones, they are still called prongs.

Head Setting

A head is a type of prong setting. It is usually a three- to six-pronged gemstone setting created separately from the main body of the ring. Many ring designs can accommodate a separately created head.

One advantage of setting your diamond in a head is that you can choose a white gold or platinum head to set off your diamond while having the rest of your ring made in yellow gold or rose gold.

This ring is set in a prong head.

Another advantage is that a head setting is easy to replace years later when the prongs get worn down.

Heads can be made for one or more gemstones and can be simple or more detailed.

Bezel Setting

A bezel setting is an unbroken rim of metal that snuggly surrounds a gemstone and securely holds it in place. The bezel setting was one of the earliest methods of setting gemstones into jewelry. Today, many beautiful and modern designs make use of bezel settings.

Bezel settings are more complex and challenging than, for example, the simpler prong setting. Bezel setting is more labor and time intensive. The pictures should help you see why: a bezel fits each gemstone's entire circumference. A prong setting can be forgiving; a bezel setting isn't.

Bezels can be slightly popped up above the main ring design or they can rise up steeply.

There is also a style called semi-bezel. In a semi-bezel setting, part of the gemstone is exposed—a very modern design with a "wow" effect.

Channel Setting

In a channel setting, a row of gemstones is set between parallel walls of metal *(the channel)*. The gemstones' edges tuck inside a groove cut into that wall.

The channel design style creates a river of sparkle or color. When you run your hand across the top of a channel setting, it feels smooth and buttery. This design is known for not catching on clothing or gloves.

Calla's Comment

Women with an active lifestyle often choose a bezel setting style because it's smooth to the touch and won't catch on clothing. Many sleek and powerful designs gain visual strength from the bezel design element.

Large diamonds can be set in a "V" channel. This gives an open and appealing side view. It makes the center diamond appear to float. It's a great way to set a center diamond if you do not want your ring to catch on clothing.

A channel setting is more protective of your gemstones and reduces risk that your gemstone will catch on a sweater or anything else in your life. A small prong just doesn't have the protective armor that the additional gold or platinum in a channel offers. The only real disadvantage of the channel setting is that it's considered a modern style of design and generally not compatible with vintage detailed designs.

Inlay Setting

Inlay setting is used with softer gemstones that are not traditionally faceted. I use a lot of lapis lazuli, malachite, and opal in my inlaid designs.

Inlay setting embeds custom-cut gemstones into a corresponding unfilled area, sometimes called the trough, within the surface of the ring. The inlaid design is made and cast in gold (or other metal), then polished, prepared, and given to the lapidary (stone cutter). The lapidary takes the chosen gem, then cuts, polishes, and sets it to fit the design. Ideally, there is a tight fit between the gemstone edges and the walls of the trough.

Calla's Comment

Elaine is a rebel and a rule breaker. Her 18-karat yellow gold and opal ring is her wedding ring. I advised against it, but made it anyway. I love its beauty, and five years later, it still looks amazing. I mention this so you'll know that the rules can be broken if you want something badly enough. If you go into your rebel design with your eyes open and an understanding of the extra care and attention your ring may need, then you have my blessing.

Because of the softness of most gems used in inlay, daily wear can be very damaging to them.

I frequently demand that my brides choose a sturdier gemstone, because I love brides and brides love their rings. I want their rings to last, and I can't help myself! I'm that jeweler who prefers not to use inlay setting for a wedding ring.

Flush Setting

A flush setting style provides a seamless look, as you can see in this chic multicolored sapphire wide wedding band. The gemstones are set down into the gold. Ideally the top of the gemstone is at the same level as the surrounding gold, or very close to it.

The flush setting works well with smaller, faceted gemstones. There's a great reason for this, and it's all about how gemstones are cut.

The wider the faceted gemstone top surface is, the taller the gemstone is from top to bottom (table to culet). If too

large a gemstone is chosen for this setting style, that gemstone's pointy culet could poke through the bottom of the ring and scratch the skin on your finger when putting it on and taking it off, or even during everyday wear. Ouch!

Pavé Setting

Pavé (pronounced pah-váy) comes from the French word for paving, pavement, or cobblestones.

It's the perfect description for this setting style because tiny gems, usually diamonds, are laid together, barely touching, much like paving stones.

One of the many pluses of the pavé setting in design is the ability to design in curves. You can create a sparkling field of diamonds that bends, goes in a straight line, or covers a rounded surface.

The jeweler works the gold after your ring has been cast, with a tool to create tiny prongs.

Alternately the tiny prongs are preplanned and are cast in your ring. Each jeweler has their special way of creating a pavé setting, and from one to another you'll often see subtle differences.

Randi's Collection of Auntie's Sapphires

When she came to me to design a ring, Randi got this funny look on her face. She practically turned away when she showed me her plastic vitamin-sized bag with some tiny, blue sapphires.

She wanted to work these sapphires into her engagement ring design. They were a gift from her jewelry-loving aunt.

The previous designs she'd been shown were either too thin or too ornate. Randi wanted a vintage feel to her engagement ring with some width to it and couldn't figure out how to use the tiny sapphires. Pavé setting them in a little triangle shape did the trick.

At the time Randi got married, she loved her engagement ring so much she couldn't decide what to do for a wedding band so she didn't get one.

For her next two big anniversaries, her husband Juan gave her a pavé-set pair of stacking rings to flank her engagement ring.

She had me solder it all together into one big ring, which she loves with a fiery passion.

SECTION THREE

CHOOSING THE RIGHT RING

The First Priority for Your Ring: Make Your Hand Look Good

Your hand isn't a mannequin upon which to dangle random rings. Hands and fingers come in as many different shapes, sizes, colors, and ages as every other part of a woman. Your rings should complement your hands according to various characteristics.

What looks good on your hand may not look so spectacular on someone else's. You need to work out what design elements present your hand in the best light and make you feel beautiful, strong, loved, however you want your jewelry to reflect the woman you are.

Beth's Story

Beth brought me a picture of her best friend's engagement ring. "I want one like this, but to be more unique I want an emerald-cut center diamond." I cringed. What would her friend think? Also her friend had different shaped fingers. That style really worked on her hand. In the who wore it better department, she'd win. Nope! I was going to fight this idea… in a nice way.

I had her try on different thicknesses of rings. The hyper thin ring shank like on her friend's ring did not look good.

"Ooh, that's not great is it?" she asked. "Not really," I said. She looked great in a ring that tapered and was angular.

Once we changed the width of her ring design, and figured out what complemented her hand, her own personal tastes flowed to the surface. We designed a great ring together. Beth not only changed diamond shapes, to a round diamond, "it sparkles way better," but she went with a blue diamond!

For all the complex and exciting parts of this adventure of designing your wedding rings, there are some fundamental tests that all rings must pass. These tests apply to wedding rings, since you'll plan to wear your ring every day, everywhere, for the rest of your life.

Ideal Shapes and Details: Discover Your Best Ring Look

Making your hand look good is all about finding the ideal shapes and details to accent your hand and fingers, just like finding the right waistline, taper, and fit for a dress.

Langella Photography

Try on different rings to see what complements your hand the most. Sammy's Jewelry House may declare that narrow rings...are the fashion-of-the-day, but does that style pair well with the width and color of your fingers? Your hands are unique. They may call for more, or fewer, details than what's featured in the latest wedding magazine.

The Second Priority for Your Ring: Hold Up to Your Lifestyle and Roll with the Punches

Your lifestyle is a player in the game of designing your ring. If you are athletic and active with your hands, a delicate design may lead to frustrating downtime for maintenance.

Your jeweler should help you choose a ring design that is strong enough for your lifestyle. If you know your ring will get some banging around, consider adding a texture or two to your design.

Textural elements are like jewelry camouflage, nicely concealing scratches and dings on your ring.

Structurally, a ring you'll wear daily needs more strength than a special-occasion ring.

Read my blog post, "Wedding Jewelry vs. Occasional Jewelry: Four Pillars of a Daily Wear Ring," and think about the lifestyle you want your ring to stand up to.

Calla's Blog
Wedding Jewelry vs. Occasional Jewelry: Four Pillars of a Daily Wear Ring

Tina's Choice, and Second Thoughts

While still a teenager, and long before she'd met Sven, her future husband, Tina had already picked out her pretty wedding ring.

From years of reading magazines and perusing jewelry store windows, she'd made her choice. It would be breathtakingly thin with a halo of tiny diamonds around the center diamond. That center diamond and halo would soar in a floaty looking way, above her hand.

Shortly after getting married, she began having reservations about whether the ring matched her hand. She hated how her super thin ring, kind of muffin-topped her finger.

Her misgivings grew until we talked one day and figured out what width would look good on her hand.

Tina looked much better in a wider, dome-shaped ring shank. A month later, Tina showed off her beautiful new wedding ring to Sven. "I love it. It looks even nicer now," he said in his Swedish accent.

Elements to Consider When Choosing a Ring Design for Your Best Look

Like the most flattering cut and shape of a dress, every dimension of a ring plays an important role in how it complements your hands.

- *Diamond Shape.* Try on different diamond or gemstone shapes and see if a particular one is more complementary than others on your hand.

- *Height.* I've learned that hands over 30 years of age often look better with a bit more height. Hands under 30 can usually go with lower profiles.

- *Size of Central Element.* Age and finger size determine overall dimension. The larger the finger, the larger and wider the center element. Larger gemstones typically look best on mature hands. Younger and smaller fingers look more balanced in smaller-sized rings.

- *Width.* The ring shank wraps around the finger and meets the main part of the design on top. Larger and more mature fingers look better in wider-shanked rings. Smaller and younger fingers can look better in narrower-shanked ones. Those with big bones should try on rings with wider shanks.

This stacking set looks wonderful on her long finger.

- *Straight vs. curved shank.* There is no hard and fast rule with regard to which looks best. My advice is to try on an assortment of both types to determine which complements your hand the most.

- *Taper vs. no taper.* Many of today's popular rings involve straight shanks descending from the center element.

  On the other hand, tapered designs can create a beautiful effect, making your hand look more feminine. Try on different tapered shanks and see if one particular straight or curving taper looks best.

This double halo engagement ring uses a tapered feature for the shank.

In addition to dimensions, the shape, size, and structure of your ring, the big elements to consider are the various techniques that create texture, color, and finish.

- *Textures and finishes.* Younger hands usually do better with smaller designs and high polish finishes. Hands over 30 benefit from textural finishes and more complex components.

- *Color. Yellow gold? Rose gold? White gold or platinum?* Warm skin tones tend to look best in yellow and rose gold. Cooler skin tones tend to look better in whiter metals. Some skin tones seem to look good in all colors! Try on different colored rings. See which color metal complements your skin more: yellow, rose, or white.

And here's that unique piece only you bring.

- *Personality.* The "X-factors" that help to determine the best size and scope of a ring are as unique as you are. Tiny rings can look unbalanced on people with big personalities. Conversely, a big bold ring can look out of place on a more reserved woman.

Choosing Your Best Metal

The higher the karat (kt) of yellow gold you use, the more vivid and yellow the color will be. If you plan to use yellow gold for your rings, try on the different karat color tones to see how they work with your skin color.

Gold is so beautiful, and it's also very soft. The higher the percentage of gold in the mix (the higher the karat), the softer your ring will be and the more prone to damage, denting, or cracking. With higher karat yellow gold rings, I like each element to be a bit thicker so it will be stronger and longer wearing.

White Gold vs. Platinum

If you love the color of white metal, you get to choose between white gold and platinum. If you think that platinum is heavier and harder than gold, you're right! But does that make platinum "better"? Not exactly. Each metal has qualities that are best for particular jewelry designs.

This is a great ring for platinum, with engraving and protected settings.

The advantages of white gold (gold mixed with alloys to make it appear white) are its lower melting point and ease of casting.

Your maintenance of white gold jewelry can be more straightforward than platinum. An annual polish and rhodium plating process can bring

This scratched and oval shaped platinum ring demonstrates the malleability and scratchability of platinum metal.

back the shine and the "bright white," making your ring look brand new.

Platinum is denser. It's tougher. It takes hand-engraving wonderfully and is great for larger gemstones and intricate designs. For some designs, platinum is absolutely the best choice, the most beautiful, and the longest-lasting.

However, platinum's melting point is much higher than gold's, almost 3,000 degrees, and special tools are needed to work with it. Platinum is more expensive at every point along the way: to purchase, to cast, to set, and to repair.

Platinum is a very malleable metal and it does scratch, and it can get dull much more quickly than white gold.

If you'd like to get a lot more scientific about white gold vs. platinum, read my blog post "White Gold vs. Platinum for Wedding Rings."

With high polish, white gold is the best metal choice for holding its shine longer.

Calla's Blog
White Gold vs. Platinum—For Wedding Rings—What's the Difference?

This ring with its many tiny prongs and super narrow shank should use the stiffer white gold.

Calla's COMMENT

If you select a ring style with white metal with a lot of plain shiny polished area in the design, you should pick white gold, as platinum with dull up faster and big areas of dull gray are not as attractive. White gold holds that shiny look longer.

What's important to know here is that your jeweler can and should help you decide which metal is best for your lifestyle and for the specific designs of your rings.

SHOULD YOU CHOOSE ROSE GOLD FOR YOUR WEDDING RING?

Rose gold has become a very popular jewelry color in recent years, for one obvious reason: it's beautiful!

I have created some lovely engagement and wedding ring sets for my clients in rose gold, and they have been very satisfied.

But I would never do that without making sure you know what you're getting into.

"Rose gold" isn't a kind of gold found in nature. It's a color created by combining gold and copper. Both gold and copper are among the softer metals, so rose gold won't hold up to an active lifestyle as well as yellow or white gold (or platinum).

Calla's COMMENT

Wilhelmina loved rose gold. Her fiancé, Mike, met with me to design her engagement ring. Having read about rose gold on my blog, he asked what we could do to set her Asscher and half-moon cut diamonds more securely. He knew she'd wear it daily and he figured it'd get banged around. We decided on yellow gold to set her major diamonds in the crown portion of her ring, with the balance of her ring to be in rose gold. I wanted to add depth and strength because it was the slightly softer rose gold. We decorated the deeper side height with hand engraving. Wilhelmina loved her ring. Years later, it is strong and has been problem free.

Another thing to be aware of is that repairing or modifying rose gold is a more challenging task for a jeweler.

As my bench jeweler says, "That copper is all mixed in with the gold, but when you heat it, the copper wants to separate from the gold and migrate to itself." This can create weak spots in a repaired ring, and because copper does change color with exposure to the elements, your ring could possibly discolor at a repair site.

If you go into a rose gold ring armed with the knowledge of what might lie ahead, you'll be extremely well pleased. I won't let you go down this path unprepared.

If you'd like more information, you can read "Rose Gold, the Blushing Gold, for Your Engagement Ring."

Wilhelmina's Two-Tone Engagement Ring

Calla's BLOG
Rose Gold, the Blushing Gold, for Your Engagement Ring

Titanium, Tungsten, and Alternate Metal Wedding Bands

I don't recommend titanium, tungsten or alternate metal wedding rings for a number of reasons. The first is... it's just not gold or platinum.

Your Magic Ring!

A wedding ring is like a talisman: an object, like a stone or a jewel, thought to bestow magical powers on the person who carries or wears it. Your wedding ring is more than just a symbol saying "I'm married." It's like the talisman—protecting the union and sanctity of your marriage and guarding against the evil spirits of divorce. You want it with you throughout your marriage.

Titanium and Tungsten Rings: Impossible to Size

Titanium and tungsten are almost impossible to size or solder. I can almost guarantee there's nobody in your hometown able to size a titanium or tungsten ring.

If you end up having a size 8 tungsten band and you need a size 9, you'll need to order it online. Because it's inexpensive you might just chuck your old one. Is that what you want to do when your finger changes size? With your wedding ring? Get a whole other ring? Nah!

Calla's Blog
Don't Buy Titanium or Tungsten Wedding Bands

Gold and Platinum Rings Can Be Sized and Soldered

Gold and platinum can be soldered and sized and worked on by jewelers. Titanium and tungsten can't. Ten years from now, when you're ten years older, you'll easily be able to have your gold or platinum ring sized larger.

Want to replace your smaller center diamond with something bigger? No problem. Need to retip your worn prongs? Again, not a problem with gold and platinum.

Know this: Your finger size will likely change over time. Even if the rest of your body doesn't, your knuckles may continue to grow. Finger sizes can easily change. As can gold and platinum rings. Titanium and tungsten rings? Nope.

Section Four

Decorative Extras

Calla's Comment

From the too plain internet engagement ring I saved with hand engraved detail, to the man's scratched ring I hammered for a cool rustic look, I've found textures and extra details to be a fun way to problem solve and upgrade rings. These extra options can make your ring sing.

Inscription vs. Decorative Engraving

Using engraving as an element in your design individualizes your ring. Engraving elevates and adds focus to your ring. It is especially cool to add symbolism in your engraving to reflect an interest or values that you share.

Inscription Engraving

Inscription engraving refers to any engraving done on the inside of a ring.

Decorative engraving is the work done on the outside surface of the ring.

Decorative Engraving

Calla's Blog
Why You Should Engrave Your Wedding Rings: And What to Engrave

Three Types of Engraving: Hand, Machine, and Laser

Hand Engraving

Hand engraving allows for one-of-a-kind designs tailored to the width and taper of your ring. The hand engraver is an artist. If you look at examples of their work, you'll know whether or not they will give your ring the finishing touches that you seek.

Hand Engraved Inscription

What makes hand engraving different from a machine or laser engraving technique is the ability of the hand engraver to make a line or curve go from narrow to wide and narrow again in one stroke. This adds a feeling of depth and interest to the design. Hand engraving is typically deeper and easier to see than machine engraving.

Hand engraving is not "machine" perfect by design; its purpose is to lend personality to the piece.

Most hand engravers can duplicate any unusual language letters or symbols. They can offer a very wide range of choices of designs because they are freehand working the motif or message into your ring.

Hand Engraving Artisan at Work

Machine Engraving

In machine engraving, a ring is held in place in a machine that includes a vise, metal templates or patterns, and a cutting tool.

The engraver sets the metal template letter or number tiles in place and follows the line of each symbol while a corresponding cutting tool engraves your ring.

Machine Engraved Inscription

The depth and thickness of the lines will be neat and uniform throughout the engraving. Because the cuts are typically shallower than those a hand engraver makes, machine engraving may not last as long.

The limitations of machine engraving include a limited number of available fonts and a generally shallower impression.

The plus point is that machine engraving looks precise and is the least expensive of your engraving choices.

For examples of the styles of engraving, you can read my blog post "Engraved Rings: Five Things You Need to Know."

Calla's Blog
Engraved Rings: Five Things You Need to Know

Laser Engraving

Laser engraving has both a computer operator and laser engraving machine.

The operator programs your message, figures out the space you have on your ring and the font size needed, and the laser machine executes your message or design.

Since beams of laser light are so small, hot, and precise, very small font size inscriptions, such as vows and other phrases, can be etched on the inside of your ring.

Laser engraving increases engraving depths by varying the dwell time of the laser beam. Dwell time means how long the laser beam is in contact with the metal at any given point. Because the dwell time can be preset for long periods of time, laser engraving can also be used on metals like titanium and tungsten, which are too hard for hand or machine engraving to etch.

Calla's BLOG
**Engraving a Kiss inside a Wedding Ring!
Laser Engraving Is Awesome!**

Design Choices and Metal Engraving Techniques

Milgrain Edging

Milgrain engraving looks like little beads of metal. It is frequently done at the edge of your ring or to frame an engraved design element of your ring.

See more pictures and a video of milgrain edging in my blog post "Milgrain Engraving Explained, Could This be Your Killer Design Detail?"

Before and After

Calla's Comment

After many years of wearing her platinum wedding band, Stacy wanted to change up her band. She felt it looked dull. With hand engraving in the scroll style and milgrain framing her emerald cut diamonds and the engraving itself, it ended up looking like a whole new ring.

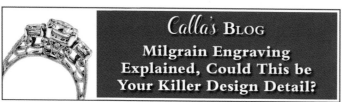

Calla's Blog
Milgrain Engraving Explained, Could This be Your Killer Design Detail?

Cast-In Engraving

Cast-in engraving is used when you want the look of decorative hand engraving, but not its higher cost. The jeweler engraves the original wax model rather than the finished metal ring, and then casts the metal.

Cast-in engraving is available on ring styles that exist as a design that can be made repeatedly. The detail won't be as crisp, but it is an option.

Cast-In Wheat Design

For a Deeper and Bolder Engraved Look

Do you want a word, symbol, or design that is very deeply engraved into your ring?

Then carving into the wax prior to casting is the way to go. Hand engraving cannot delve very deeply into gold because of its hardness.

The side-wall lettering was carved into the wax before casting.

Finishing Techniques That Can Make Your Ring Look Stellar

You can have a simple design that with finishing touches becomes more unique. If you've struggled with the thought of wanting simple lines, yet a unique design, this section may inspire your solution.

CHOOSING TEXTURES AND FINISHES TO ADD PERSONALITY TO YOUR DESIGN

Textures add spice and personality to jewelry. A number of choices exist for setting off your gemstones and expressing yourself.

When used in combination, different textures can create a greater feeling of three-dimensional depth for your ring.

Varying textures from large to small elements also greatly affect the final look. Here are some textural choices to consider in your design.

Hammer Finish

Imagine striking the surface of a ring all over with the tiny rounded head of a specialized jeweler's hammer to get a hammered finish look.

The width and depth of the indents will vary depending on the size of the tool.

With a solid band, the whole surface is typically hammered, giving the ring an organic, rustic, and often, masculine feel. With other ring designs, this finish can be used as a partial element in combination with others to give it a unique look.

For guys who are hard on their rings, consider choosing a nice thick metal to hold up to the slings and arrows of life and think about a hammer finish so when you scrape it while lifting, you're merely adding to the patina and beauty of your rustic or textured ring.

Matte Finish

In matte finished jewelry, the surface of the metal is scuffed and abraded, making for a frosted, less-shiny appearance.

Different tools and techniques are used to achieve subtle differences in the finish. Sandblasting is one of the techniques in which fine particles of sand are "blasted" at the surface of the jewelry, creating a very uniform matte look.

Other matting techniques can impart a varied rustic matte finish. A small matte finished section of jewelry can impart striking contrast and a three-dimensional depth when used alongside an area of high polish. Consider using a matte finish around little diamonds in such an area to make the stones sparkle and pop.

Satin Finish

Satin is the subtlest of the matte finishes. A "satin" finish is a term often used to refer to a softer, almost pearl-like gloss.

Stipple Finish

A stipple finish is achieved by carefully hitting the surface of jewelry with a steel punch. This deep and well-ordered texture gives a very strong appearance and looks great next to intense colored gemstones, sparkly diamonds, or high polished metal.

High Polish

A smooth, shiny, mirror finish is called high polish and is the most popular of all textural components. Consider adding a bit of matte finish to make the high polish sections really pop.

Oxidation

In jewelry making, oxidation is the process of darkening the surface color of metal by applying a chemical substance.

This dark finish is typically used in nooks and crannies in order to create sharper borders and highlight contrasting areas.

Oxidation is not permanent and will need to be reapplied from time to time.

Enamel

When you want a color, like black for an accent, to set off your gemstones or add interest to a design feature, one of your choices is enamel. For daily-wear rings, I like to design with enamel as the detail, not the star. I like to protect it by recessing it a bit. One of the great things about enamel is the huge choice of colors.

Twig Finish

One of the finishes I like is the twig finish. Looking at an actual twig, I use a tool to scrape the gold after casting or the wax of the ring before casting. Many textures you see in nature can be replicated in metal if you wish. Just know that the more rough and random a finish you create, the more frequent cleaning it may need to look good.

Three twig textured stacking rings, one with black rhodium plating.

Plating, the Secret Technique That Can Elevate Your Ring

No jewelry design book would be complete without a discussion of plating. Plating can be done for effect, to alter the vibe of your ring, or for maintenance.

The term "plating" is actually short for "electroplating." Without getting technical (or boring you to death!), electroplating is the process of covering one metal with a thin layer of another metal. The item to be plated is immersed in a chemical solution containing the covering metal, electricity is added, and, by the process of electrolysis, the suspended molecules of gold, or whatever you are plating, are transferred onto the piece of jewelry.

Rhodium

The most common plating material is something you may never have heard of: rhodium.

Rhodium is a rare, naturally occurring member of the platinum group of metals. It's extremely hard. It's silvery in color and highly reflective. It doesn't corrode and doesn't react with most chemicals. These properties make it ideal for plating.

Before rhodium plating on white gold ring.

After rhodium plating on white gold ring.

We use rhodium to plate white gold jewelry. Because of the very bright and shiny nature of rhodium, it gives white gold a more defined and bright white.

More often than not, white gold pieces of jewelry you see in jewelry stores have been rhodium plated. It's the final step in the creation of most white gold jewelry.

Black rhodium plating on the matte finish floor makes the gem colors pop.

The reason you should know about it is that part of the white gold maintenance routine includes replating your white gold ring with rhodium when it loses that bright white look.

Black Rhodium Plating

When I discovered the black rhodium finish, it allowed me to design in a more edgy way. Thanks to a client who wanted that antique-y, darker look to her ring, I was inspired to find out how to achieve it.

Drummer Brian Chooses Black Rhodium

That rock 'n' roll look that black rhodium gives to a ring feels fresh to me. When death metal band White Chapel's drummer chose my black rhodium trinity ring for his fiancée, I knew that it was not my imagination.

An example of black rhodium with hand engraving.

Calla's Blog
Rhodium Plating;
Like Coloring Your Hair,
Only for Jewelry!

Can You Black Up Your Wedding Ring?

That plain white gold shiny band you're thinking about wearing that you'd like to spice up with black rhodium? Uh, no. That won't fly one bit. What makes black rhodium "stick" to your jewelry is a textural or three-dimensional element.

If you choose a design with black rhodium, make sure that you have a jeweler nearby who can occasionally replate it. If not, you'll need to mail your ring away to get this work done.

Alternatives When You Want Dark Gray or Black Details

For a more three-dimensionally defined look, or antique finish, see other techniques, which include oxidation and enamel, in my blog post.

Black rhodium makes your diamonds pop.

> **Calla's Comment**
>
> When I started using hand engraving in my designs years ago I felt that same excitement. It's the discovery that an added element contributes more than you thought it would. With black rhodium there's just something so rock'n'roll and slightly misbehavin' about it. I just love that!

Calla's Blog
The Kiss of Night for Your Jewelry
Using Oxidation, Black Rhodium and Black Enamel

Yellow Gold Plating

Yellow gold plating, puts a fine coat of yellow gold over the metal you are plating. The plated yellow gold is often brighter than the underlying gold.

Before and After

If you are momentarily blinded when you first see your newly gold-plated ring, know that this brighter yellow tint will calm down with time.

Higher karat gold plating such as 18kt gold or higher can look kind of orangy. I'm a fan of 14kt color. Sometimes someone brings me a piece of jewelry to show me the color they want it to be. All I can say is we can't tinker with the color. Just know it may initially be quite bright looking.

Rose Gold Plating

Rose gold plating is generally asked for if your rose gold ring has darkened. I had a hairdresser client who had certain chemicals that turned parts of her rose gold wedding ring quite dark. We plated her ring at least yearly.

Because the rose gold plating has a lot of copper in it, the color will darken a bit over time. Since rose gold has that high copper content, that translates into rose gold plating being the least stable of the gold plating colors.

Two-Tone Rings and Plating

Over the years many of the people I've worked with have had two-toned rings. Some of these rings were cast in both yellow and white gold or platinum, which is ideal.

This ring's maintenance includes both white rhodium plating and yellow gold plating.

However, some people discovered that their two-tone ring was merely plated a different color in certain areas and called "two tone." Bummer.

The good news is that, by replating those faded areas that were once yellow gold, the two-tone aspect of your ring will stand out like new again.

Even rings cast in two separate colors of gold benefit from gold and rhodium plating to really separate the two colors and sharpen their look.

One of the attractions of using more than one metal color in your ring is that it creates a more three-dimensional look.

The texture in the center will hold the rhodium plating longer than a high-polish finish.

Plating and Your Ring's Maintenance

Rhodium plating is a necessary part of your white gold ring's maintenance. For older yellow gold rings, you'll find that they can develop a dowdy look. Sometimes yellow gold plating is just what the doctor ordered to bring back a brighter yellow look.

With your black rhodium-plated ring you'll need to replate it when it becomes faded or scratched.

Reviving that new look for your ring is where plating excels. It makes your ring look shiny, bright, vivid, and new.

Black rhodium plating for the area holding the black diamonds creates drama.

SECTION FIVE

REDESIGNING FROM AN EXISTING RING

Why Redesign?

Do you have a ring you're not wearing? Does it feel out of date? Maybe you're tired of the way it looks or your personal style has changed. If the gemstones are special to you, it may be a piece well worth redesigning.

Carol's Redesign

I share this story because there are many ways to get to your wedding rings. One of them is to start with gemstones you already have and create something new.

Carol had an outstanding ruby in a ring that she hadn't worn in years. Her tastes had changed and the ring just wasn't seeing the light of day anymore. She's also a collector of antiquities.

We discussed her new style, which was now bolder with bigger outlines, and decided on a freeform Etruscan style. The Etruscan design style is one of the earliest jewelry designs in history, so this idea spoke to her.

What sets the Etruscan style apart are its high outer walls of gold protecting the details in the lower floor of the ring, along with high pop-up bezels that hold and protect the gemstones.

Carol's diamonds differed in shape and size. The previous design didn't showcase the differences that noticeably. She and I both agreed that highlighting their differences would be key to an interesting ring.

This was a fun and challenging design. I decided to set the ruby at an angle because the asymmetric outline of her ring wouldn't work with the standard up-and-down center gem orientation. The gems ended up looking like they were floating. This looks so cool on her hand and celebrates her strong, fun, and independent personality.

There were remaining diamonds left from Carol's original ring. We used them to make a contoured band that paired well with her main ring. The mixed shapes of her diamonds were alternated across the top and halfway down the sides for standalone or worn-together versatility.

What I loved so much was her story of going to Las Vegas with friends and wearing the two rings knuckle to knuckle together for the first time. Vegas is over the top glitzy anyway and she had strangers coming up to her and loving her ring. Her ring became a conversation starter about a shared love of history and antiques.

Julie's Wedding Ring from Grandma's Diamonds

Julie was a doctoral student and she and her boyfriend Ron, of five years, wanted to get married. As starving students, they didn't have much of a budget for rings. Julie's grandmother gave her a ring and said, "You can use this."

As a white metal wearer, Julie didn't quite know what to do with her gift. We decided to reuse the diamonds only. Because of her very active lifestyle she wanted the opposite of her grandmother's prong-tastic design. She wanted a smooth feel that wouldn't catch on anything.

Being an artistic person, she wanted art, beauty and a flowing feel that would set her grandmother's diamonds and yet be very much her taste. Ron was very happy that we were figuring out Julie's ring.

Julie's grandmother was so pleased with the new design holding her old diamonds. Julie's ring became not only her wedding ring, but a very happy connection with her grandmother.

CHRISTINE AND SAM'S 25TH WEDDING ANNIVERSARY REDESIGN

Not all who design a dream ring are newly engaged. Christine loved her engagement ring for years. She loves David Yurman silver and gold jewelry too. As her 25th anniversary got closer, she told her husband she'd love to redesign her ring in yellow and white gold.

Sam thought that'd make a memorable 25th anniversary gift and said go for it. What started out as discussing how to show the two colors of gold morphed into finding themes in the jewelry she wore regularly. She loved the bolder wider look we were designing as her fingers had changed over the years and that width was quite complementary to her hand.

The only problem was that her diamond was looking smaller. Adding a halo around her diamond created the balance we needed for her original center diamond. Christine looks great in her new wedding ring.

Before

After

Marlo and Ben and the Family Diamonds

Marlo and Ben weren't supposed to get together. His "I say what I think" style of communication felt rude to Marlo. He thought she was stuck-up. They were unfortunately, or was it fortunately, paired on a project at their university.

Before, rings like these were given to Marlo.

Being forced to work together they learned how not to set each other off. And by the time they were done with the project, they were not looking forward to it ending. So they picked fights that prolonged their final write-up until Ben kissed Marlo.

That led to their happy courtship.

When Marlo and Ben told the family they were going to get married, their families were very pleased. Two different relatives on Ben's side contributed diamonds for Marlo's rings.

Ben's mom Candice was visiting when Marlo, Ben, and I sat down to design their rings and see the family diamonds. Candice was trying hard to pretend she was reading a book, but that didn't last. Pretty soon we were all together talking ideas, looking at the rings I was showing for inspiration.

Ben suggested a science fiction motif and asked if I could draw something. Marlo wanted a classic design with prong settings to let the light in all around her beloved diamonds. I'd heard the stories, but Ben was cool with Marlo's choices.

Kacie Jean Photography

Marlo and Ben's Wedding Rings

Ben wanted to keep his wedding band simple because of his work in the lab. But he wanted some aspect of his ring to go with hers.

Since Marlo's ring had a vintage feel, he chose milgrain engraving to border his high polished white gold band.

Ben cracked jokes and was a lot of fun. Seeing Candice's occasional eye rolls was priceless.

Having her soon-to-be family give her diamonds for her wedding ring made Marlo feel warmly welcomed by them.

SECTION SIX

CADs and Waxes, What You Need to Know

Creating Your Design Concept, Making Your Dream Ring Reality

> ## Calla's Comment
>
> Let's assume that after all this reading you have a general idea of what your dream ring looks like. It's time to get it down on paper with its various notes, details, and measurements. Don't worry if you can't draw well, you can still get your information down as a start to your dream ring.

THE DRAWINGS

When the basic idea is figured out between you and your jeweler, your jeweler will draw a picture or two or three to show the details that you've discussed. Some jewelers charge for and create a fine art image of your ring.

That's not my style. I draw pictures to illustrate a curve here, a height there, to show how this diamond will be set and where that little filigree detail will go.

In a two-dimensional way, the drawing or drawings should show you that your jeweler gets that you want a rounded top on your ring, not a flat top with sharp edges. The drawings shouldn't be about beauty, but about features and your individual detail desires.

It's important to have a top view of your design, the shank view, and the gallery view.

The CAD Computer-Aided Design

The views you want to see in your CADs.

An important step is the creation of your wax model. Your jeweler may choose to create a CAD, computer-aided design mock-up.

CAD mock-ups are like a "wireframe" of your ring, detailed as far as form, height, and shape go. These CADs are used as the pattern to 3D print your wax model.

Be warned, CADs are ugly. See examples of CADs and finished rings in my blog post.

The finished ring from the above CAD images.

Calla's Blog
Ring CADs Can Look Ugly—Ring Design and Your CAD

Hand Wax Models

Another option is to have your wax model hand carved. Your jeweler will decide whether the design wax you want should be drafted with CAD and 3D-printed, or hand carved.

A good two-dimensional drawing is no guarantee that your preferred details are understood.

CAD representations are very technical, a "wire frame" of something beautiful. But the wax itself is truly three-dimensional, and the closest representation of your ring before it is made.

Hand Carved Wax and Finished Ring

CAD image and finished ring; note how tall the prongs are in the CAD.

I recommend approving the wax or CAD model before casting the piece in metal. This step is especially crucial with intricate or complicated rings. It's better to make changes in the CAD or wax model than to see your finished ring with a flat surface when you requested a domed look and it's too late.

Intricate details like special finishes and engraving will typically be added after the ring is cast in metal and, thus, will not show up on the wax model.

Six Features to Look for in a Wax or CAD Model

1. Check for depth, especially around the shank. Rings worn daily should be thicker than those worn for special occasions. If your ring will be worn beside another, make sure its height matches its mate. Discuss with your jeweler, too, if the width is appropriate for the size of your finger.

2. Check the edges for roundness or angularity, depending on your preference.

3. Oftentimes, you won't be able to gauge how high your gemstone will be set just by looking at the wax or CAD model.

The prongs may appear twice as big as they need to be. Don't despair. Tinier elements like prongs are regularly exaggerated in the wax to ensure a proper casting, and then filed down afterwards.

Calla's COMMENT

Lonnie and Merika wanted a ring that showed the detail of swords of strength and love from their favorite video game. The level of detail wasn't on offer in their town so they chose an out-of-town jeweler who showed other rings with that level of detail. That jeweler was me and it was a fun and challenging ring to create. Look at the work your chosen jeweler has done and that'll let you know that they can give you what you want in the detail department.

Discuss how high or low you want your diamond or gemstone set. Point out an example you admire of setting height in one of your jeweler's rings.

4. Check the taper of the shank. Make sure it reduces in width to your liking.

5. Make sure the inside curve on a comfort-fit shank is slightly convex. Comfort-fit shanks move more smoothly over the knuckles. Water dissipates more easily from between ring and finger too.

6. Check the fine details of the gallery. The gallery is the side view under the central top part of a setting. Good galleries add uniqueness and beauty to a ring. Design techniques include filigree, engraving, and open work designs.

This is a gallery view.

Final Words on What You Are Looking For

Channel your inner engineer, not your inner artist, when examining the wax or CAD model. Pay attention to the dimensions: height, width, and curve of the shank. Make sure the shape is what you requested. Ignore prongs that stick too high up, as they get filed down after being cast in metal.

SECTION SEVEN

ALL ABOUT YOUR HANDS

Getting Your Finger Sized, the Right Way

First, get your finger sized by a jeweler who knows their business. Trying to do it yourself with a string or strip of paper is risky, at best.

Those plastic sizers that are adjustable that you get in the mail aren't as accurate as I'd like either.

Jewelers measure fingers with metal ring gauges, called ring sizers. These are sets of metal rings ranging in sequential sizes from small to big sizes. If you're needing your own ring sizer, purchase one online.

Calla's Comment

If you've never worn a ring before, there is a tendency to choose a size that is too big because it seems "comfortable." Guys are especially good at this. More guys lose their wedding bands fishing or swimming than women. Maybe it's because women are not that into fishing? Nah. Your ring can fall off in cold water when your finger shrinks. Make sure you have a snug fit over your knuckle.

Wide Band Ring Sizers vs. Narrow Band Ring Sizers—They Make the Difference

Be aware that there are wide ring sizers for finding the correct size for wide rings and narrow ring sizers for measuring finger sizes for narrow rings. Narrow ring sizers are about 3mm in width; wide ring sizers about twice that.

Wider wedding bands usually require a slightly larger ring size. You'll want to use a wide band sizer to ensure a good measurement.

For example, if with a narrow band sizer you are a size 8, a narrow ring should fit fine on your finger. But if you are buying a wider band, you will probably need more like a size 8½.

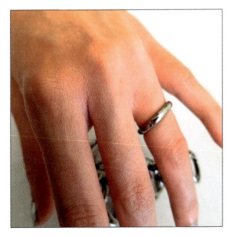

Narrow Band Ring Sizer

Wide Band Ring Sizer

Four Things Not to Do before You Get Your Finger Measured for Size

1. Work out. It makes your finger bigger.
2. Eat salty chips or a lot of salt. It makes your fingers bigger.
3. Eat a bunch of apples. They make you lose a lot of water weight, making fingers smaller.
4. Do strenuous work with your hands. It makes your fingers bigger.

Five Reasons Why You Still Might Get a Wrong Size

1. Humidity enlarges your fingers.
2. Heat enlarges your fingers.
3. Cold shrinks your fingers.
4. Your fingers go up and down in size during the day and during the month.
5. If you take medication, that can affect your finger size.

Fit Feel, What's Too Tight and What's Too Loose?

You may have a particular tightness or looseness that you're most comfortable with in the fit of your rings.

It's an important thing to know about yourself because your jeweler will measure your ring to the tightness *they* like.

It may not be the feel *you* like. For best results, communicate your preferred "fit feel" to your jeweler whenever resizing your rings and when having custom-made rings created.

Guys, Resist the Urge to go Loose in Your Ring Size

If you guys have never worn a ring before, you'll gravitate toward a loose fit. Just know that's too loose for a ring you'll wear every day.

Try on the half size smaller than your comfortable size and see if it's constricting, or merely snugger. Pick a fit that requires a bit of a tug to get over your knuckle, but isn't tight once past the knuckle.

Medium Fit

Too Loose

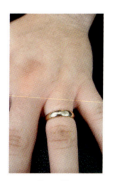

Snug Fit

Figuring Out Your Girlfriend's Finger Size

Ask her best friend, her mom, or sister. If they don't know her size, they may figure out a way to find out. They'll probably greatly enjoy being part of this happy adventure.

If you can take a ring she wears on her right-hand ring finger to a jeweler (she probably doesn't have a ring for her left-hand ring finger since that is the wedding ring finger), they can put it on a ring sizing pole, called a mandrel, and tell you the size of it.

It's a good guess that her left-hand ring finger will be smaller than her right-hand ring finger. A safe guess would be to make her engagement ring a half size smaller than her right-hand ring size.

Choose a design that can be easily sized after your proposal to fine-tune the fit.

She will love it, even if it doesn't fit.

Calla's COMMENT

If you don't know her size, make her ring anyway. Guess high, as a woman would rather size her ring smaller than have to size it larger. We love to be surprised with that loving forever ring.

Don't Despair, Solutions for Rings That Spin and Big Knuckles

If the difference in finger size between your knuckle and the area between your knuckle and your palm (where the ring sits) is too great, you'll find you cannot get a satisfying fit for your ring.

I call the difference between the size of your knuckle and the size of your finger where your ring rests, the "knuckle-to-finger differential."

This measurement is the key to understanding that there may be a problem and what to do about it.

An above normal size differential can send a ring spinning around your finger.

A flexible ring sizer is used to determine your knuckle-to-finger differential.

Beth's knuckle is two sizes larger than her finger. We have put in a hinging shank so she can get it on.

Lori's Wedding Ring Dilemma

Lori's knuckles had increased in size over the years to a point where she couldn't wear her rings anymore. They would flop from side to side if sized large enough to slip over her knuckle. If sized according to the base of her finger, her rings wouldn't fit over her knuckles. Yikes!

Lori found that butterfly springs kept her rings upright.

Is This You?

If you've ever had any of these problems, don't despair, solutions exist!

Before deciding which possible solution might help you, your knuckle-to-finger differential needs to be figured out. I made a video that shows you how to figure out your knuckle-to-finger differential.

The butterfly spring on lori's ring grasps her finger firmly and comfortably.

Calla's Blog
How to Figure Out Your Knuckle-to-Finger Differential for Rings

Three Solutions

1. **Speed Bumps**. Speed bumps are little balls of gold or curved gold pieces soldered to the inside of the bottom of a ring. These raised elements of metal often gently anchor into the fleshy part of the finger helping to keep your ring upright and keep it from spinning.

2. **Butterfly Spring**. A butterfly spring is a flat piece of metal soldered to the inside bottom of your ring. It spreads outward as the ring goes over your knuckle and springs inward once it is past your knuckle. Each butterfly spring is custom made based on the size and width of your ring.

Butterfly Spring

3. **Hinging Shank**. A hinging shank opens and closes at the bottom, or side depending on the style chosen. It allows the ring to slip easily over the knuckle when open. Once in place, behind your knuckle, the ring is snapped closed at the base or side of your finger. Several different styles exist. Talk to your jeweler about which might best fit your needs.

Finger Mate Hinge

Horseshoe Shank

Other Options: Horseshoes and Squares

Squaring-off or widening the bottom of the ring can be effective in better anchoring your ring. Creating a horseshoe-like bump-out can also be helpful. Talk to your jeweler about a solution that might work well for your hand and ring style.

Square Shank

Which Solution Is Right for You?

Those with a one-size knuckle-to-finger differential are good candidates for speed bumps. A butterfly spring is usually better for those with a one to two size differential. The hinging shank is most beneficial for those with differentials beyond two sizes.

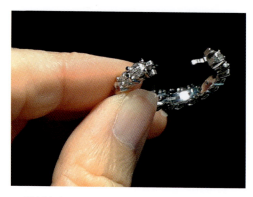

CLIQ's hinge open solution that works with eternity bands and men's band rings.

It's Your Dream, You Deserve to Wear It

Don't let large knuckles rob you of your dream ring design. You deserve to wear the ring design you love and not settle for something practical because you banged up your fingers playing volleyball for years. Once you've designed your dream ring and figured out your knuckle-to-finger differential, you can have the solution that will work best on your hand designed into your ring.

Epilogue

After a movie, Jeremy and I and our son Dan were walking down State Steet. A woman pushing a stroller next to a man carrying a cute curly-haired toddler called my name.

I didn't recognize her at first. "Felicia?" I asked.

"Yes! We're here for a visit. I'm so happy to see you."

"Are these your two kids?"

"Yes. Do you remember Marco?"

"Yes, I do. Hi, Marco."

"Felicia gets so many compliments on her rings," Marco said. That just made my day.

We chatted awhile and it was just the coolest thing seeing her again and seeing her beautiful family.

Felicia inspired this book!

Your Dream Made Real

Wedding rings mean different things to different people. For some, wearing something meaningful is essential—as if the piece were a talisman or lucky charm. For others, it's the way to reconnect with relatives and bring family treasures into the present in a personal way.

For others, engagement and wedding rings can mean terror and anxiety! I hope this book has helped to stem some of that, and increase the excitement, anticipation, and joy that these rings signify.

Regardless of how you arrive at your dream ring, you'll know that wearing something you worked to create, makes your ring more precious to you both.

My personal dream gets fulfilled with every story I hear, of accepted engagements and happy marriages. There are, after all, few steps more important than choosing your life partner. I hope that this book helps you feel more confident and more empowered as you find your style and design your dream ring or your true love's dream ring.

Appendix

Quizzes

QUIZ ABOUT YOUR WEDDING BAND FOR THE GUYS

What is your favorite metal?
- Platinum?
- White Gold?
- Yellow Gold?
- Rose Gold?
- A Two-Tone Metal Combo?
- A Tri-Gold Metal Combo?
- Alternate Metal? Titanium, etc.? *Just Don't!*

What is your favorite width range?
- 4-5mm?
- 5-6mm?
- 6-7mm?
- 7-8mm?
- 8-10mm?
- 10-13mm?

What is your narrow band size?

What is your wide band size?

Do you like flat inside?

Do you like comfort fit inside?

Do you like flat top?

Do you like dome top?

Do you want straight angular sides?

Do you want more rounded soft edge sides?

Do you like interesting metal braid, etc., laid into your band?

Do you want to set in a row or two of diamonds or gems?

Do want to work a design special to you and your fiancée in your band?

Do you like a shiny finish?

Do you like a matte finish?

Do you like a hammered finish?

Do you want a custom texture on your band?

Do you want an engraved design or accent on your band?

Quiz about Your Engagement Ring Design for the Women

What is your narrow band left finger size?

What is your wide band left finger size?

What is your favorite metal?
    Platinum?
    White Gold?
    Yellow Gold?
    Rose Gold?
    A Two-Tone Metal Combo?
    A Tri-Gold Metal Combo?
    Alternate Metal? Titanium, etc.? *Just Don't!*

Do you have a folder, Pinterest page, etc., with pictures of the details of the styles you love?

Does your fiancé know where these ring dream ideas live? Does your best friend?

What is your favorite width range for the widest part of your ring and shank?
    2 3mm?
    4-5 mm?
    6-7mm?
    7-8mm?
    8-10mm?

Do you want your center gem or gems set high, medium, or low?

Do you want a single center gem?

Do you want a three-stone center design? (Other?)

Do you want a halo?

Do you want a straight shank?

Do you want a curved shank?

Do you want a split shank?

Do you want a tapered solid shank?

Do you want side diamonds going down the shank?

How far down the shank do you want your side diamonds to go? Half way, three quarters?

Do you like a flat inside?

Do you like comfort fit inside?

Do you like a flat and angular look on the shank where no gems are set?

Do you like rounded and dome curves on the top plane where no gems are set?

Do you want straight angular sides?

Do you want more rounded soft edge sides?

What setting style do you want for your center gem?
    Prong?
    Bezel?
    Other?

Do you want an open, see-through gallery? (That side view under the center gem or gems.)

Do you want gems set within the gallery? (Facing sideways, perpendicular to the center gem.)

Do you want engraving on the gallery?

Do you want to work a design special to you and your fiancé into your ring?

Do you like a shiny finish?

Do you like a matte finish?

Do you like a hammered finish?

Do you want a custom texture on all or part of your ring?

Do you want any dark contrasting areas on your ring? Oxidation, black enamel, or black rhodium?

Do you want hand engraving on the shank beyond the set side diamonds?

Do you want hand engraving around your side diamonds on the shank?

Will you design your engagement ring to have room for a straight wedding band in the future?

Will you design your engagement ring to go well with a contoured band in the future?

Will you wear multiple stacking rings with your engagement ring in the future?

About the Author

Calla Gold is a jewelry designer and owner of Calla Gold Jewelry. She has been a personal Jeweler in Santa Barbara since 1983. Her wedding ring designs grace the hands of hundreds of happily married couples.

Calla has been cheerfully married to Jeremy Gold since 1979, and they have a cool son, Dan.

Visit her website at **www.callagold.com** and become a fan of her jewelry on Facebook.

Acknowledgments

Many thanks to my clients for letting me share images of their designs to educate future jewelry lovers everywhere.

To my mentors, Ed Balian, Mark Mikaelian, Esteban Lopez, and women in jewelry who have helped me, Peggy Jo Donahue and Ann Glynn.

My early readers Christine Logsden, Penelope C. Paine, and Gail Kearns.

Photo Credits

Brilliant Images

Diamond Graphics

Gemological Institute of America

Kacie Jean Photography

Langella Photography

Pro Photo LA

Rick Logsdon Photography

Wikimedia Commons

Willa Kveta Photography

Index

A
Accent stones 10
Alternate metal wedding bands 49
Anniversary band 23

B
Bezel setting 30, 31
Black rhodium plating 63, 65, 66
Butterfly spring 95, 96, 98

C
CAD 5, 6, 81, 82
CAD model 82, 83, 85
CADs 79, 81
Cast 6, 32, 34, 45, 46, 63, 68, 82, 83, 85
Cast-In engraving 59
Channel setting 31, 32
CLIQ hinge 98
Comfort fit 17, 104, 106
Computer-Aided Design 5, 6, 81, 82
Contoured Wedding Rings 19
Crown 9, 48
Custom jewelry design 4, 80

D
Decorative Engraving 54

E
Enamel 63, 66, 107
Engagement ring 7, 10, 14, 15, 16, 18, 19, 22, 35, 38, 48, 75, 92, 105, 107, 108
Engraving 3, 6, 9, 14, 18, 46, 54, 55, 56, 57, 58, 59, 77, 83, 84, 107
Eternity band 18, 20, 21, 98

F
Finger Mate Hinge 97
Flush 33

G
Gallery 10, 80, 84, 107
Gemstone basics 10
Gold 5, 7, 17, 30, 32, 33, 34, 44, 45, 46, 47, 48, 49, 59, 63, 64, 65, 67, 68, 69, 72, 75, 77, 96, 103, 105
Gold plating 67, 69

H
Halo 17, 41, 75, 106
Hammer finish 60, 61
Hand engraving 18, 55, 59, 107
Hand wax model 82
Hattie's Bonus Ring 22
Head setting 29, 30
High polish 44, 61, 62, 77
Hinging shank 94, 97, 98
Horseshoe shank 97

I
Inlay setting 32, 33
Inscription vs. Decorative Engraving 54

K
Katryn's Contoured Wedding Band 19
Knuckle-to-finger differential 94, 95, 98

L
Laser engraving 55, 57

M
Machine engraving 55, 56, 57
Matte finish 61, 62, 104, 107
Milgrain Edging 58

O
Oxidation 62, 63, 66, 107

P
Pavé setting 34, 35
Plating and your ring's maintenance 69
Platinum 5, 17, 30, 32, 44, 45, 46, 49, 51, 64, 68, 103, 105
Prongs 3, 9, 10, 29, 30, 34, 47, 51, 82, 83, 85
Prong setting 29, 30, 76

Q
Quizzes 103, 105

R
Redesign 75
Redesign from an existing ring 72
Rhodium 45, 64, 65, 107
Rhodium plating 45, 65, 68, 69
Ring basics 9

Ring settings 27
Rose gold 17, 30, 44, 47, 48, 103, 105
Rose gold plating 67

S
Satin finish 62
Shank 9, 10, 38, 41, 42, 43, 80, 83, 84, 85, 97, 98, 105, 106, 107
Sizers 88, 89
Sizing 91, 92
Solder 16, 35, 50, 51, 96
Solitaire 7, 15, 29
Speed bumps 96, 98
Split shank 106
Square shank 97
Stacking bands 21
Stipple finish 62

T
Tapered shank 43
Textures 6, 44, 54, 60, 63
Titanium 49, 50, 51, 57, 103, 105

Tungsten 49, 50, 51, 57
Twig finish 63
Two-Tone Rings 68, 103, 105

W
Wax model 5, 6, 59, 81, 82, 83
Waxes 79
Wedding band 14, 17, 18, 19, 33, 35, 49, 77, 89, 103, 107
Wedding ring 2, 7, 8, 14, 19, 28, 33, 39, 41, 46, 47, 49, 50, 66, 67, 72, 74, 75, 77, 95, 100
White gold 17, 30, 44, 45, 65, 66, 68, 69, 75, 77 103, 105

Y
Yellow gold 30, 44, 45, 68, 69, 103, 105
Yellow gold plating 67, 69